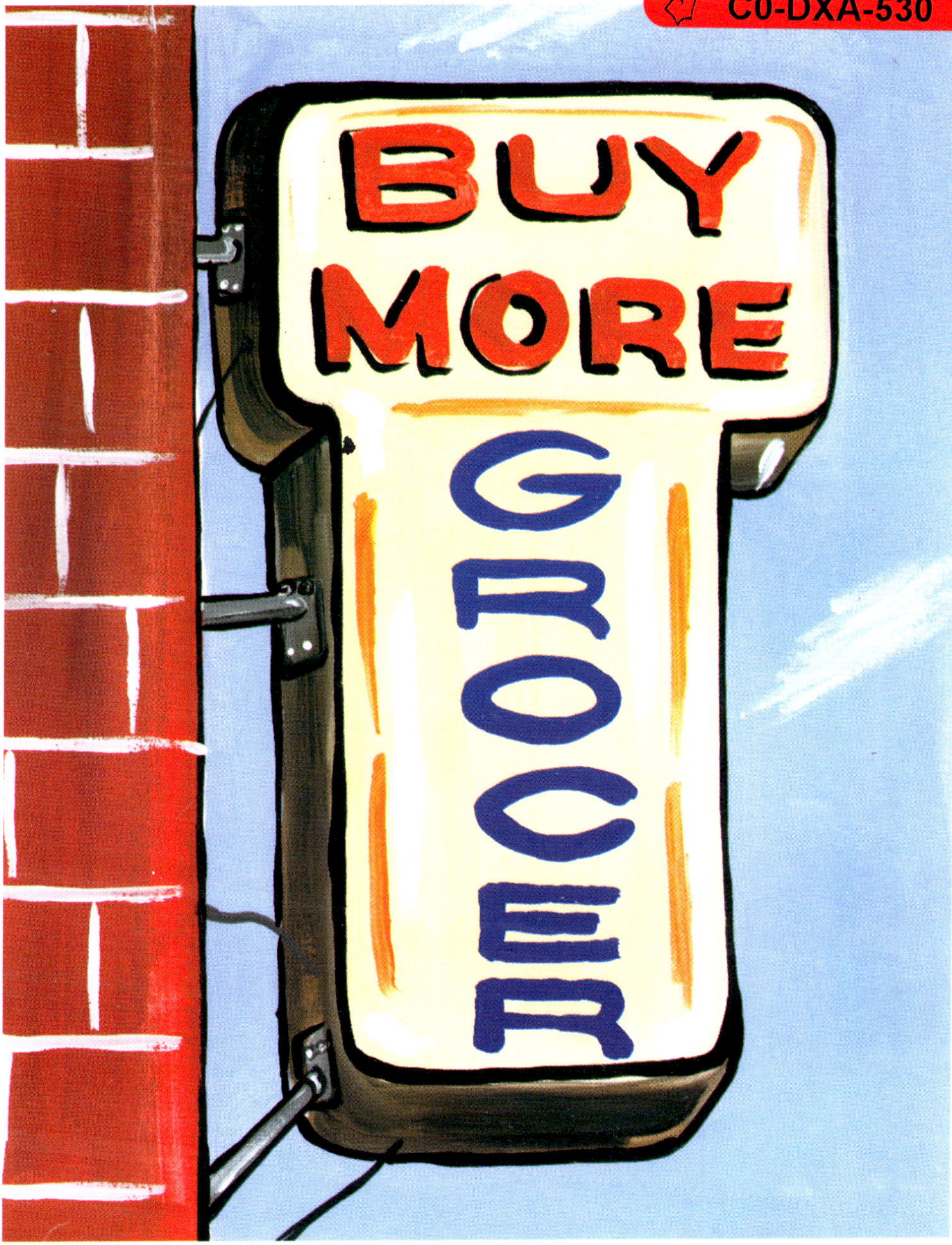

At the store we buy...

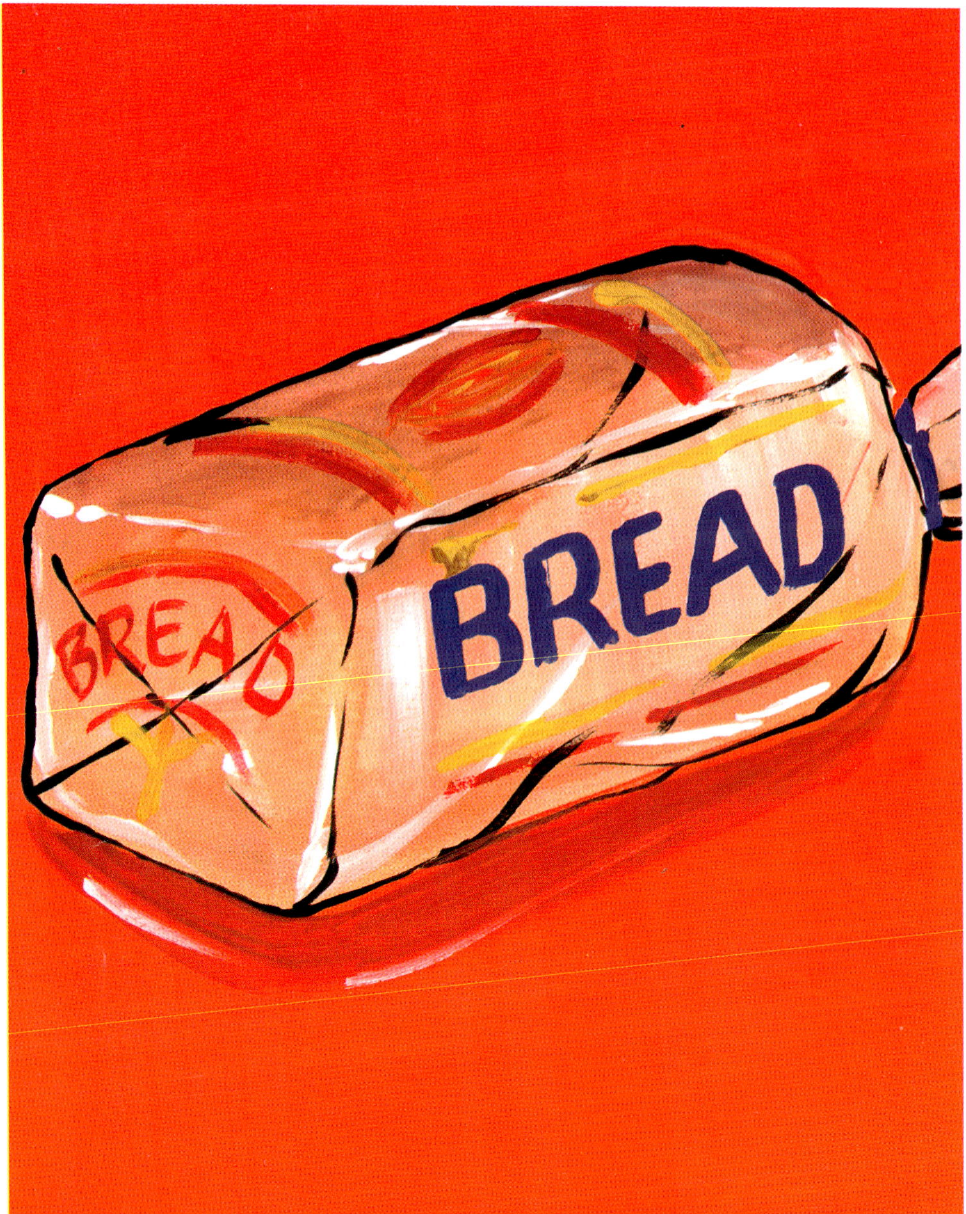

bread,

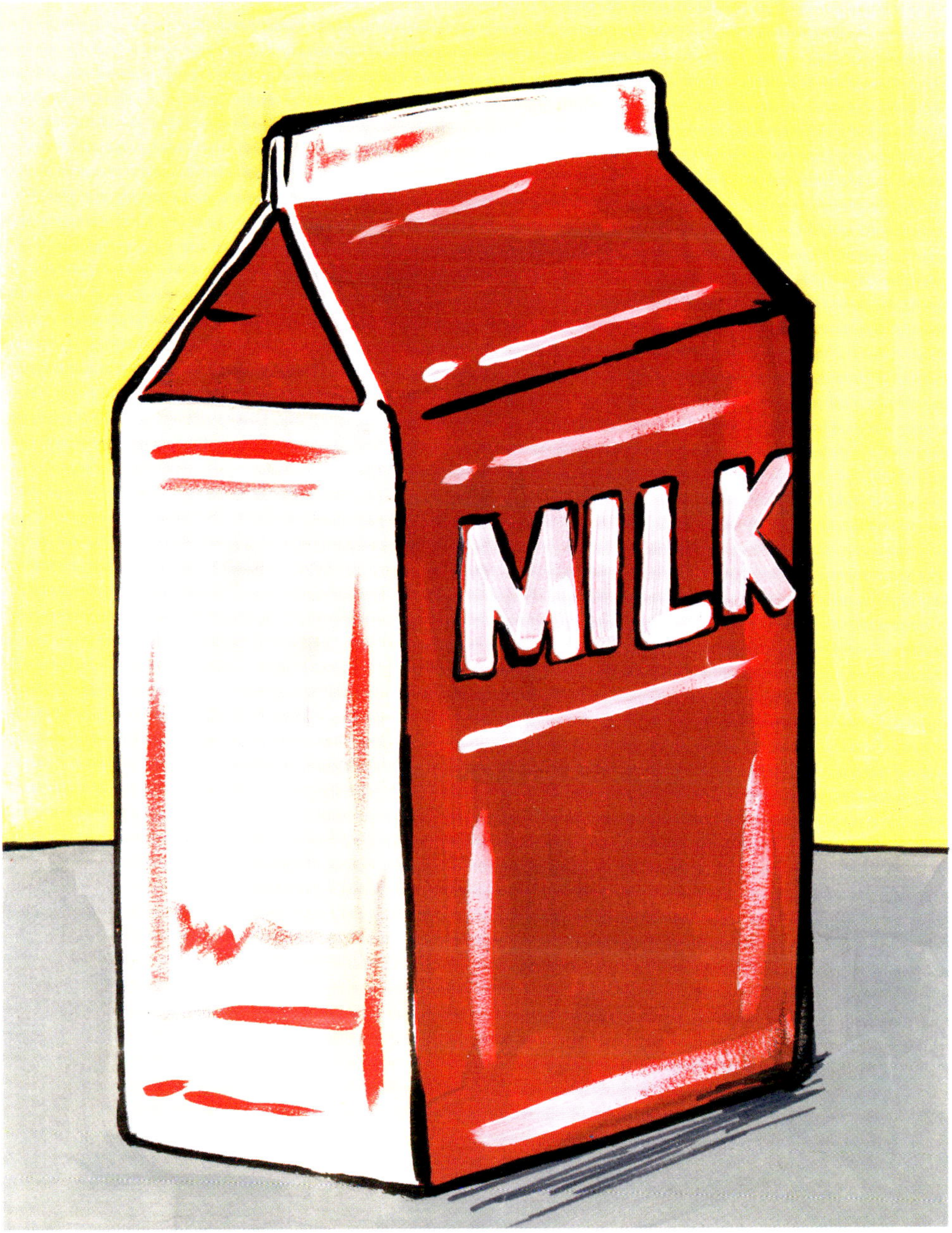

milk,

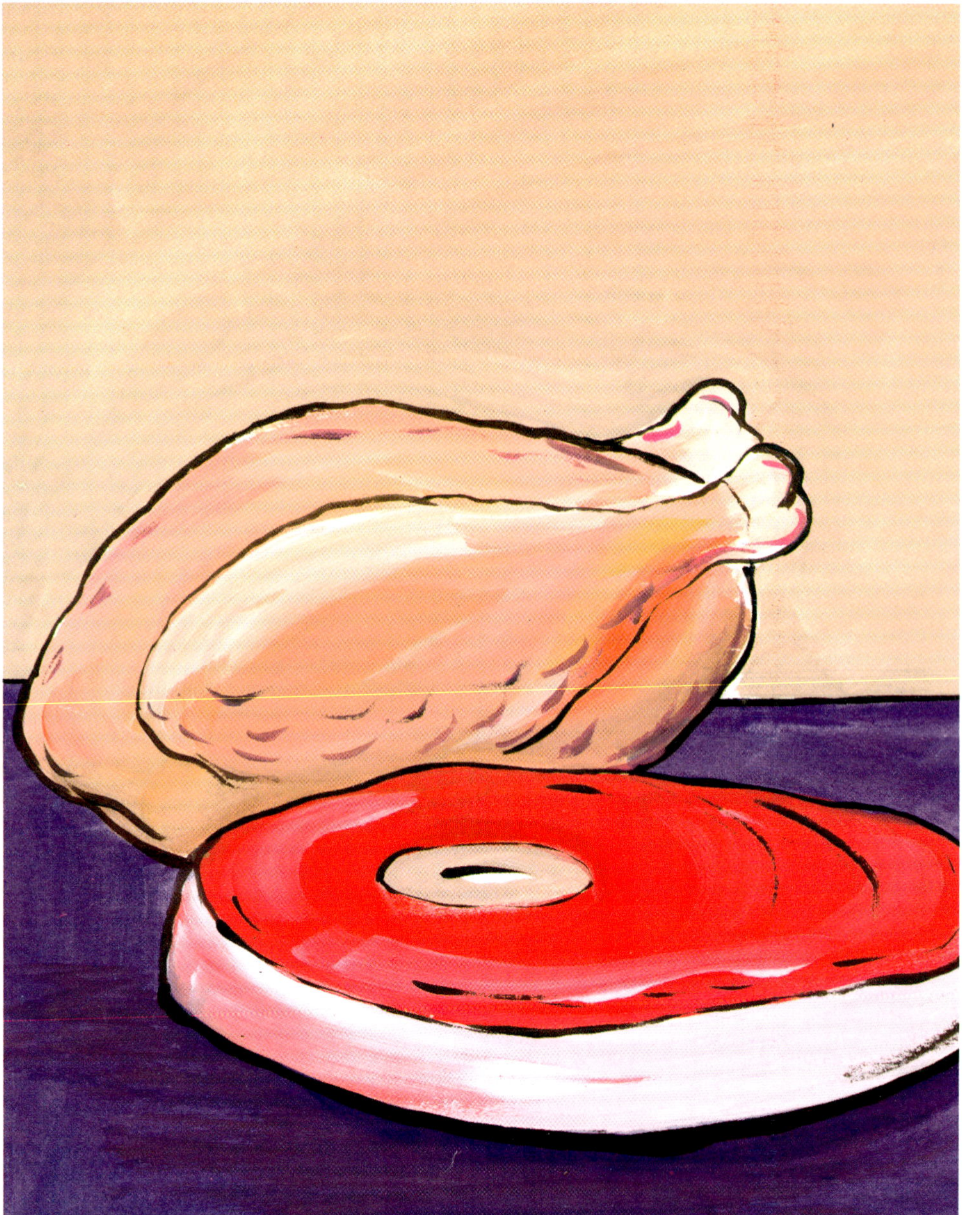

meat,

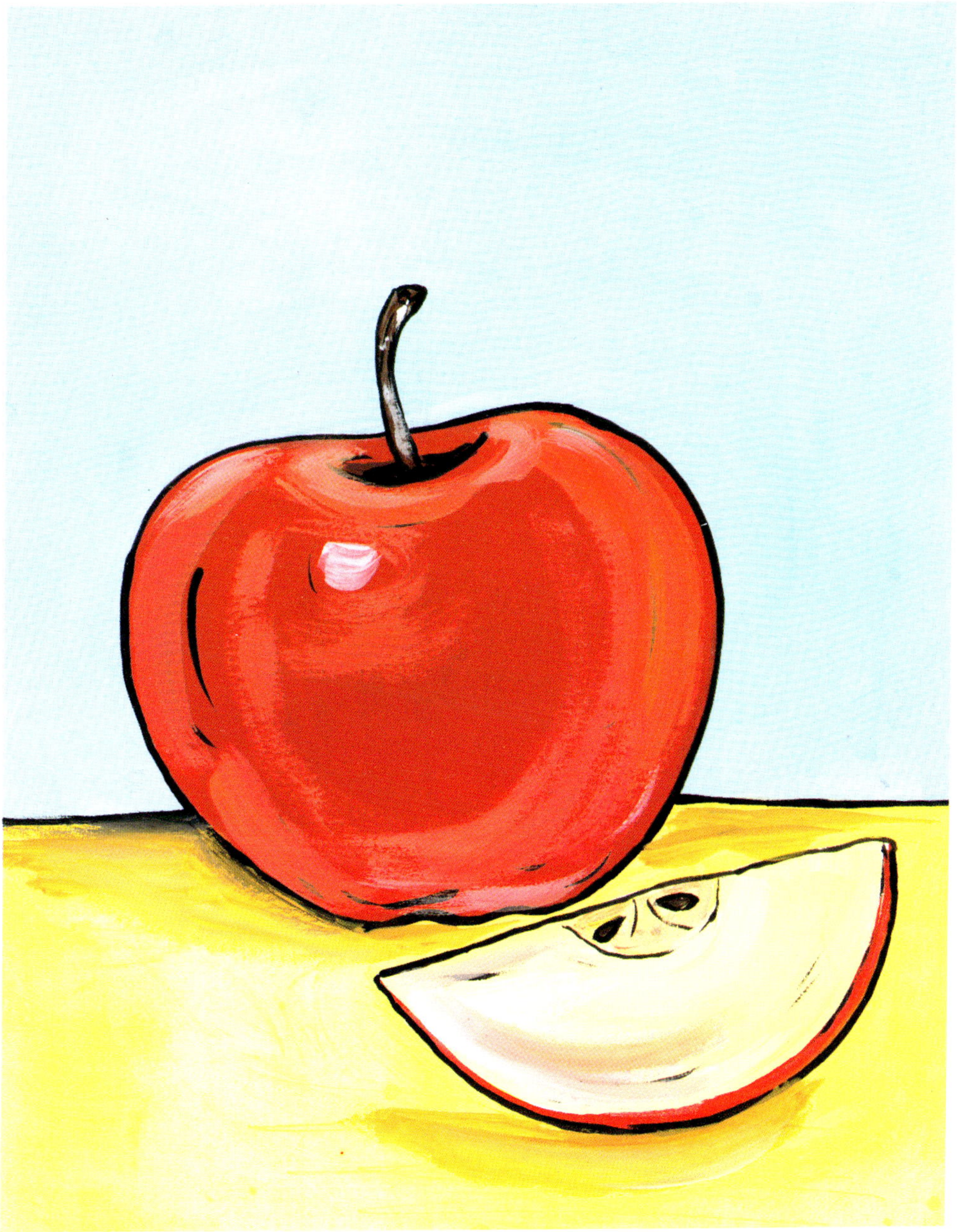

apples,

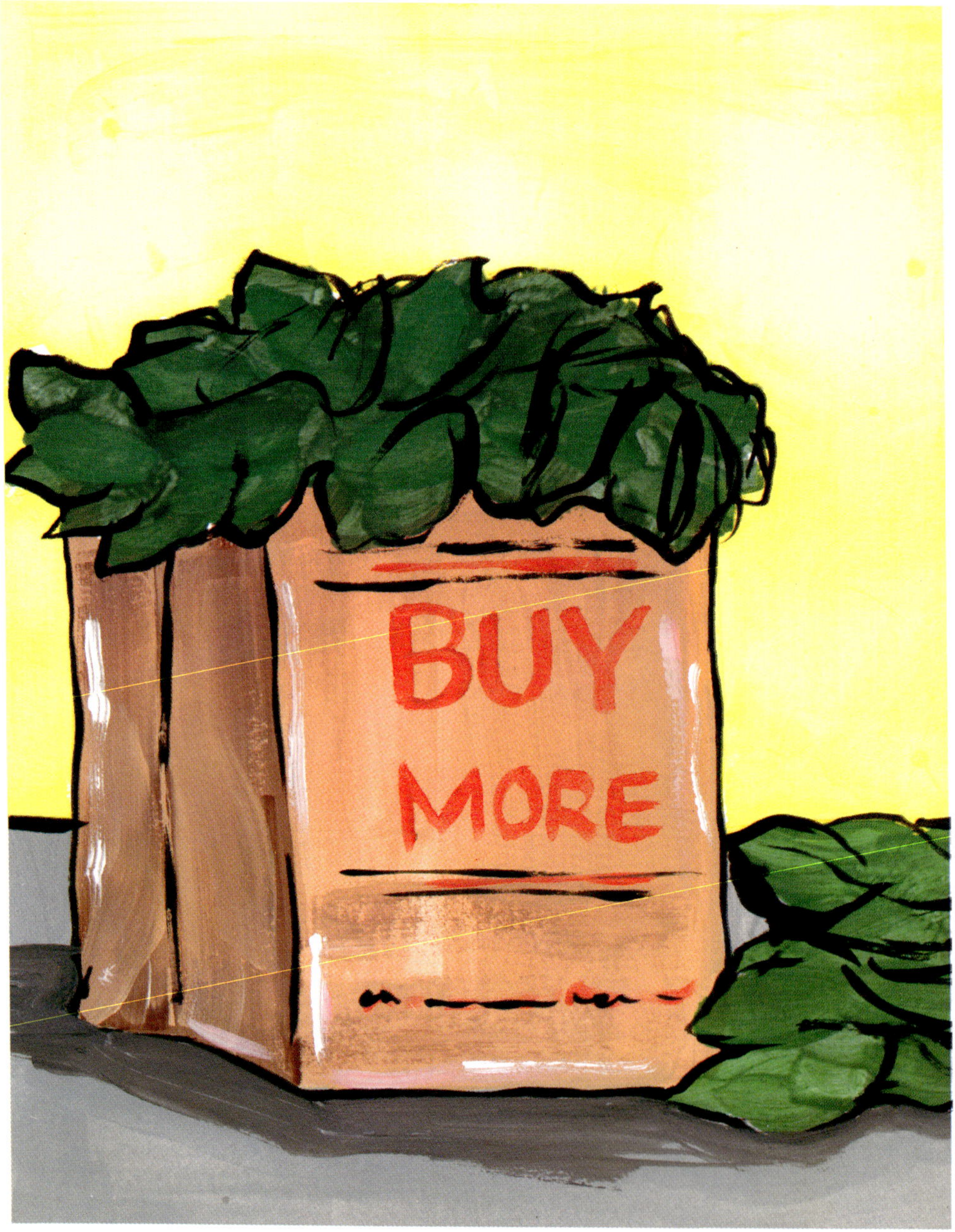

greens,

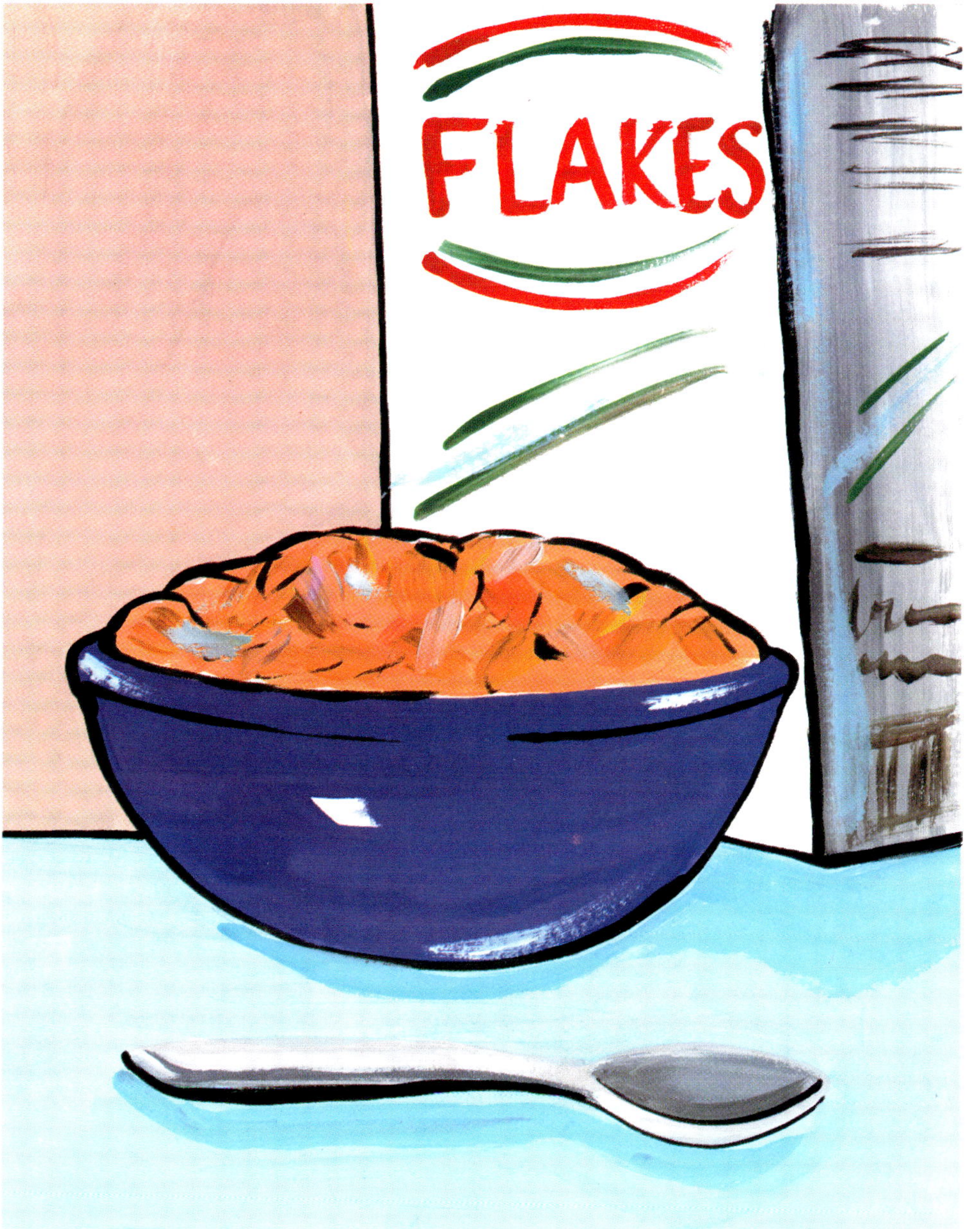

cereal

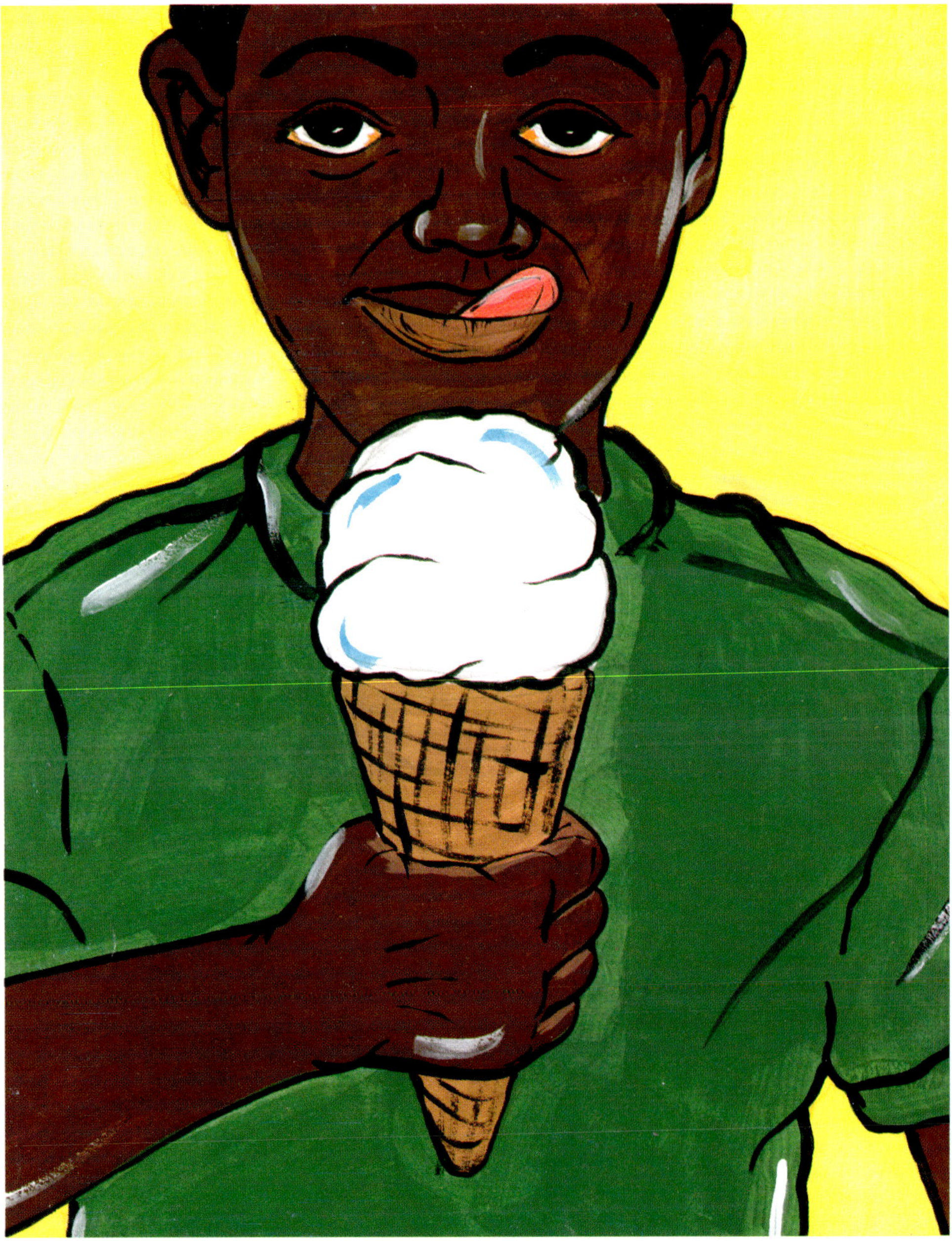

and ice-cream!